Harry Potter Spell Book: The Unofficial Book of Magic Spells

By: Sadler Mars

Harry Potter Spell Book

Aberto: Use this spell to open your kitchen cabinets instead of bending down and smacking your head on the counter. Also useful for opening doors, windows, and barbeques.

Accio: Point your wand at a small object or animal and this charm will summon it toward you. Makes stealing candy from a baby that much easier, just make sure you don't accidently grab the baby.

Aguamenti: This spell will cause water to blast from your wand like a miniature fire hose. Used in case of dragons or microwave accidents.

Alarte Ascendare: Blast your target into the air like you shoved him in a cannon and lit the fuse and said, "Adios, fella."

Alohomora: A spell that unlocks something. Mostly used on doors and windows, but sometimes cast on websites that have been blocked by annoying IT people at boring corporate jobs.

Anapneo: Cast this on your toddler when she's choking to death on a hotdog because your brother-in-law pushed her off some bleachers and the hotdog got jammed in her airway.

Anteoculatia: Ever wonder if your teacher or your mother-in-law might look better with antlers instead of hair? Let's make it happen.

Anti-Cheating Spell: Cast this on a final exam so the students don't all copy from the smartest person in the class. Can also be cast on Facebook if you think your wife's been talking too much with her ex.

Aparecium: This spell will reveal hidden text like invisible ink or those secret messages web designers hide by making the text the same color as the background.

Arania Exumai: Make spiders go away. For people with irrational fear of spiders and a love of mosquitos and flies.

Arresto Momentum: Use this spell to decrease the velocity of an object, like a baseball, or a brick that's flying at your window.

Arrow Blaster: Ever wanted to launch a hundred arrows from your wand? Now you can. For one easy payment of $2.99.

Ascendio: Used to levitate yourself up, up, and away. Useful for escaping dangerous situations or sneaking in to your girlfriend's bedroom after her parents fall asleep.

Avada Kedavra: This curse will kill your target instantly and is the most efficient way of getting rid of pesky heroes, tax collectors, and door-to-door salesmen. (One of the three unforgiveable curses.)

Avis: Summon a flock of birds that flies out of your wand and poops on your enemy's car. The birds can do other stuff, but the poop is the most annoying thing about them.

Baubillious: Distract your enemies with an ordinary and rather boring beam of light.

Bedazzling Hex: Used to create cloaks of invisibility, and also as an explanation for why you showed up at a wedding without a date. "She's over at the bar getting drinks. You can't see her because she's invisible."

Bluebell Flames: With this spell you can summon waterproof fire that glows blue and burns things that are directly above it. A great substitute for kerosene stoves and whoopee cushions.

Bombarda: Create a small explosion that can burst open locks and get you banned from flying on airplanes.

Bombarda Maxima: A more powerful version of *Bombarda* that can blow up brick walls. Only to be used in emergencies like when your mother-in-law shows up unannounced on Superbowl Sunday with her DVD collection of *Gossip Girls* and demands the television so she can bond with your wife.

Brackium Emendo: This spell can heal broken bones but not a broken heart.

Bubble-Head Charm: Create a large bubble of air around your head so you can breathe underwater or fart in a small room without having to smell it.

Calvario: This spell will cause your target's hair to fall out, and has put most wizard bikini waxers out of business.

Cantis: Aim this spell at someone and cause them to start singing uncontrollably. Avoid using on teenage girls unless you want to hear that *Frozen* song for the 11 billionth time. You just watch. In a few years that's all they're gonna be singing at karaoke night.

Carpe Retractum: Envelop your target in rope and pull them toward you. Useful for game night and college parties.

Cauldron to Sieve: Punctures your target with a thousand little holes. Mostly used on a cauldrons but can also be used on soup bowls.

Cave Inimicum: This spell is used to warn the caster of any approaching danger. Cheaper than an alarm system and more discreet than a giant three-headed dog.

Cheering Charm: Used to make people happy. Cast this on your friend who earns minimum wage and spends all his disposable income on alcohol.

Colloportus: The locking spell. Can be used to lock doors, chests, closets, windows, computers, safety deposit boxes, and fantasy football picks.

Colloshoo: Glue your target's shoes to the ground and laugh manically as they try to make a run for it but instead they trip fall on their ugly faces.

Confringo: Causes your target to burst into flames and then explode. If you're visiting America and the border agent asks if you know this spell, then you should probably just play dumb.

Confundo: This spell will cause your target to stumble about, confused and disoriented. Like maybe he just got a concussion. (Has a reduced effect on NFL players.)

Conjunctivitis: Curse your enemy's eyeballs and they will experience great pain and be unable to see you when you sneak past them.

Container Enlargement Spell: Magically enlarge a bag, trunk, or suitcase so that it can hold much more than it appears to. Useful for sneaking a case of beer into the movie theater or maybe other stuff too.

Cornflake Skin: Causes your target's skin to look and feel like cornflakes. Not the cheap stuff either. The good brand with the rooster on the box.

Cracker Jinx: Summon a plate of wizard crackers. Caution: wizard cracks may explode.

Cribbing Spell: Used to cheat on tests and exams. Will reveal the correct answer *most* of the time.

Crinus Muto: Cast this on your hair to change its color. Great for hiding from the Ministry of Magic or blending in at Burning Man.

Crucio: This curse will cause the pain of a thousand burning knives on your target. This is one of the "unforgiveable curses" and if you cast it then you're going in the wizard clink.

Cushioning Charm: Summon an invisible cushion which is great for broomsticks and the chairs at your grandmother's house.

Deletrius: Disintegrate something, especially something annoying like a house elf that won't clean the bookcases because he's allergic to dust.

Densaugeo: Aim this at someone and watch their teeth grow right out of their head. Can also be used to grow back teeth.

Depulso: The banishing charm (opposite of the summoning charm.) Cast this on something and send it far away from you. Can be used to cheat at baseball if your wand is big enough.

Descendo: Causes something to fall/collapse, or magically descend to the ground. Useful for magical staircases or making a wall fall on somebody you don't like.

Deprimo: Create massive downward pressure directly above an object. Used to make holes in floors or to flatten meat for people who are afraid of mallets.

Diffindo: The shredding charm. Use this spell to poke a hole in a bag or box. Can also be used to dispose of important documents.

Diminuendo: Causes your target to shrink. Be careful where you aim this or you might end up getting divorced.

Dissendium: Used to open secret tunnels or hidden passageways. Now you can explore the catacombs under London without getting lost and eaten by rats.

Disillusionment Charm: Gain the color-shifting powers of a chameleon and hide from your enemies in plain sight.

Draconifors: Temporarily transform someone into a dragon. If cast on a dragon it might turn it into an uglier dragon which would make it angry and then it might barf a fireball in your face, so probably don't do that.

Drought Charm: Used to remove of puddles, ponds, or root beer you just spilled on your freshly-washed pants. Will not work anything larger than a pond.

Ducklifors: Have you ever wanted to turn someone into a duck? Now you can. Aim this at your enemies and watch as they flap and quack and stumble about like morons begging for bits of bread — which is actually quite bad for ducks because bread is basically junk food. It fills them up and they don't get the nutrients they need to grow big and strong.

Ears to Kumquats: Turn your targets ears into kumquats. A kumquat is an orange that's shaped like an olive.

Ebublio: Channel the amazing power of bubbles and cause your target to explode into thousands of bubbles. Note: This spell requires a second wizard also casting a water creation spell.

Engorgio: Causes your target to grow immensely in size. As opposed to the shrinking charm, this one is actually quite popular amongst married wizards.

Entomorphis: Launch this spell at someone and turn them into an insect. Don't squash them though because that would be murder.

Episkey: Use this spell to heal a minor injury, like a broken nose, a stubbed toe, or a level 2 paper cut.

Epoximise: Magically glue two things together. More powerful than gorilla glue which is not made by gorillas despite what the commercial leads you to believe.

Erecto: Instead of wasting precious time assembling your tent like some stupid Muggle, cast this spell and watch your tent magically assemble itself.

Evanesce: Make something tiny vanish temporarily. Great spell to cast on mice and then drop down the back of someone's shirt. (Don't do this if you want to date this person someday.)

Evanesco: Cast this spell on an object and it will vanish completely from existence. Don't tell your teacher you "accidently" cast this on your homework because she won't believe you.

Everte Statum: Blast your target backward like they were swatted by a giant invisible hand.

Expecto Patronum: Use this spell to summon your Patronus, a spirit guardian. It will usually take the shape of your favorite animal, or an animal you share similar characteristics with. Mine is a cow that drank too much fermented milk and just stumbles around mooing and complaining. What's yours?

Expelliarmus: Knock the weapon out of your opponent's hand, or even blast him off his feet if you're feeling especially powerful.

Expulso: Cause something to explode like a pressure cooker with too much junk in it.

Extinguishing Spell: Mostly used for putting out fires, but can also be used to wake somebody up.

Featherweight Charm: Lower the mass of an object to make it easier to carry. Don't cast this on a planet or you're gonna have a real bad day.

Ferula: Summon some basic first aid materials, like bandages, gauze, splints, and ointments. Good spell to learn if you plan on joining the circus or eating fire for a living.

Fianto Duri: Increase the strength of your shield spells. Cast this on your starship if you ever run across a Borg Cube.

Fidelius Charm: Use this charm to hide top-secret information inside the soul of another person. It can also be used to protect a secret location and that location will appear invisible to all but the secret keeper.

Fiendfyre: Create a swath of uncontrollable fire that will burn though anything in its path, even a horcrux. If you're out camping and you see a sign that says: ABSOLUTELY NO BURNING, it's probably a good idea not to cast *Fiendfyre*.

Finite: Use this spell to remove all other spell effects from someone. Much less slimy than kissing a frog.

Firestorm: Summon a ring of fire that blasts out of your wand and incinerates your enemies.

Flagrante Curse: Curse an object so that whenever someone touches it they will be horribly burned.

Flagrate: You ever wander into a wizard bar and see the restaurant's logo burned into the wooden tables? The *Flagrate* spell is how they do that.

Flame-Freezing Charm: Causes fire to tickle instead of burn and is a much more efficient way of dealing with a burning building. Muggles dump water on it and ruin all their belongings.

Flipendo: Knock your target back a few steps. The more powerful a wizard you are, the farther back your enemy will be knocked.

Flying Charm: This charm may be cast on flyable objects like broomsticks and magic carpets. It also works on cars although if you steal one and crash it into a tree you're gonna have a bad day.

Fumos: Summon a cloud of dark smoke that hides you from your enemies.

Furnunculus: Causes your target to break out in a terrible case of acne.

Fur Spell: Use this on anybody you think might look hilarious if he were covered in fur. You can also trick Muggles into thinking they just saw Bigfoot.

Geminio: Creates a non-magical replica of an object. Example: If Indiana Jones had cast this spell on the idol in that first temple in *Raiders of the Lost Ark*, he wouldn't have triggered the trap. But if Indy had cast this spell on the Ark of the Covenant and then opened it, nobody would have gotten their faces melted off.

Giant Toenails: Causes your target's toenails to grow extremely fast and extremely large and long. Very gross. Don't cast this on yourself unless you're trying to set a world record.

Glacius: Transforms a person or object into a solid block of ice.

Glisseo: If you ever wondered how great it might be to turn your staircase into a slide, now you can find out.

Hair-thickening Charm: This charm will save you money on wigs, toupées, and hair extensions.

Herbifors: Aim this spell at someone and watch as flowers burst out of their skin.

Herbivicus: Helps plants grow up quickly to their maximum potential. Be careful when using on pumpkins and sunflowers.

Homenum Revelio: If you think there's an invisible human in your room spying on you, cast this spell and it will reveal them.

Homonculous Charm: Create a magical map and track the movements of everybody in your chosen area.

Homorphus Charm: Restore a transfigured object or person to its original shape.

Horcrux Curse: This spell will allow a dark wizard to transfer part of his soul into various objects so that he may (in theory) live forever.

Hot Air Spell: Causes your wand to spew out hot air and is useful for drying clothes and inflating hot-air balloons.

Hour-Reversal Charm: Turn back time by up to five hours, but be warned, this charm is highly unstable and if you cast it then things will probably not end well for you. I mean think about it. If everybody could just run around turning back time when they didn't like how the cookie crumbled then the world would be a huge mess and nothing would ever get done. Don't play around with this. If you feel you absolutely *must* go back in time in order to rectify some horrible mistake then try and limit yourself to only a few minutes, or just do what everybody else does: live with your bad decisions, get a therapist, and self-medicate with junk food.

Hover Charm: Causes an object or person to levitate for a few minutes. Very useful spell for competitive games of The Floor is Made of Lava.

Hurling Hex: Cast this on a wizard's broomstick and it will shake back-and-forth and up and down and try to hurl whoever's riding it into the air.

Illegibilus: Use this on anything with writing and it will blur the text to make it unreadable by even the sharpest of eyeballs.

Immobulus: Prevents a person from moving, twitching, or itching.

Impedimenta: If something dangerous is running toward you and then cast this spell on it and they will trip and fall on their ugly faces.

Imperio: One of the "unforgiveable curses." This will allow you to control the mind and actions of your target and they must do everything you say. A great source of cheap labor.

Imperturbable Charm: Cast this spell on a door and nobody will be able to pass through it or eavesdrop through it. Can also be used to seal bottles, cans, or anything with a stopper.

Impervius: This charm will make an object act as though it were coated in a special substance that repels all other substances. For example if you cast this on your clothes and then go running in the rain, your clothes will be dry when you get home.

Incarcerous: Casting this spell on someone will cause them to be tied up in magical ropes. This spell gets more fun as you get older.

Incendio: Create a small fire so you can use floo powder or get people to pay attention to you.

Intruder Charm: A more efficient security system than an alarm but not as fluffy as a dog.

Locomotor Wibbly: Causes your target to trip and fall.

Jelly-Brain Jinx: Makes your target dumb. Cast this on someone who always beats you at games of Scrabble or Boggle and have fun smashing their puny score.

Jelly-Fingers Curse: Turns your target's fingers into jelly which makes typing vhery hhharadd,

Lacarnum Inflamarae: Shoot a ball of fire from your wand. In most video games and fantasy stories a spell like this would be called *Fireball* which is a lot more self-explanatory than *Lacarnum Inflamarae.* It's almost as if the wizards are trying to make casting spells intentionally difficult to keep magic out of the hands of outsiders. In the real world that's called protectionism/stupid-doctor-handwriting, and generally thought to be bad economic policy. (I suppose the counter-argument is they make spell-casting difficult to keep it out of the hands of people who might use it for evil, but if that's the case, then why are they letting people who are too young to vote, drive, or drink, launch incendiary weapons from their wooden sticks?)

Langlock: Cast this spell on someone and their tongue will be magically-glued to the roof of their mouth and they will have difficulty speaking, mumbling, or doing other fun things.

Lapifors: Use this spell to turn your bedside lamp into a rabbit. Who needs a bedside lamp these days anyway? If you're a wizard you can just create some light. If you're a Muggle then you're probably reading this on a device that generates its own light. (This spell also works on small things that aren't lamps, although before casting *Lapifors* you should consider the environmental ramifications of introducing magical rabbits into your local biosphere.)

Legilimens: The mind-reading spell. Browse through your target's memories, thoughts, and emotions like magazines on a rack.

Levicorpus: Dangle someone in the air, upside down and by their ankles. To free someone from this spell, you can cast *Liberacorpus*.

Locomotor: An object-levitation spell. In order to cast this spell you must also name the desired object. For example if you want your favorite block of cheese to follow you around all day, you would say *Locomotor Cheese.* If you're in a deli you should probably be more specific or you'll cause a scene.

Locomotor Mortis: Lock someone's legs together preventing them from moving. Considered a red-cardable offense by most football/soccer referees. Pretending you've had *Locomotor Mortis* cast on you is a common strategy to get a penalty call in your team's favor.

Lumos: Turn your wand in to a flashlight/torch that produces light. The louder you yell "Lumos!" the more light you'll get. *Warning*: This is not cool light. *Lumos* will produce some amount heat so if you stab your homework with your lumosified wand you might light it on fire.

Lumos Solem: Produce a ray of light that's as bright as the sun. Whatever you do, don't intentionally aim this in someone's eyeballs or you're going to the headmaster's office for tea and shouting. In fact, don't even cast this unless it's an emergency. What do you need super-bright sunlight for? Open a window. You're a wizard. There's a hundred spells you can use to open windows or blast a hole in the wall. Get creative.

Melofors: Turn someone's head into a pumpkin. (They can still talk, but you can't bring them out to dinner or they might wind up as dessert.)

Meteolojinx Recanto: If it's raining outside and you suspect this bad weather is the result of magical tampering, cast this spell and everything will go back to normal. If it's still raining then it was just raining. Sometimes that happens. It's best not to get too worked up about it.

Mimblewimble: This spell will curse someone so when they try to reveal your secrets their tongue curls up in their mouth and they can't talk. They could always write it down though, so maybe instead of cursing people you could just keep your secrets to yourself.

Mobiliarbus: Use this spell to levitate and move a simple object.

Mobilicorpus: Cast this spell on a corpse and you can move it around with your wand. It's not exactly a zombie so don't get any evil ideas about world domination. It's more like a really stinky puppet.

Mucus ad Nauseam: Sort of like the opposite of the cure for the common cold. Cast this on someone and your target will experience symptoms like a runny nose, headache, sleepiness, drowsiness, and if they go to the movies they will cough during all the good parts and everyone will hate them.

Muffliato: This spell will cause people who are trying to eavesdrop on your conversation to only hear a dull buzzing instead of whatever top-secret wizard stuff you're talking about with your awesome wizard buddies.

Multicorfors: This charm will change the color of your clothing and is much cheaper than buying a new wardrobe every time the season changes.

Nox: This spell will extinguish the light produced by the *Lumos* spell.

Oculus Reparo: This simple spell will fix a broken pair of glasses.

Obliteration Charm: Destroys footprints and internet browsing history.

Obliviate: This spell can be used to wipe someone's memory and is surprisingly *not* an Azkaban-punishable offense. You could do some pretty evil things to someone and then wipe their memory. They did it all the time in *True Blood* and it was generally not for friendly purposes.

Obscuro: Causes a blindfold to appear on your target's eyes. Great for when you need to make your mutinous crew walk the plank.

Oppugno: If you're having an argument and you feel like you're losing but don't want to admit it, just cast *Oppugno* and your opponent will be attacked by whatever simple-minded animals are nearby.

Orbis: This spell will cause your target to sink into the ground like they're standing on quicksand. A great tool for negotiating a discount on a furniture purchase.

Orchideous: Instead of hiding a bouquet of flowers up your sleeve like some ugly Muggle, cast this spell and a bouquet of flowers will magically appear from your wand.

Packing Spell: Command your luggage to pack itself.

Patented Daydream Charm: This charm will give someone a super-realistic daydream that lasts about 30 minutes. In the Muggle world this charm is called acid, only the daydream is usually unrealistic. Also, acid is illegal, and dangerous, and very hard to find especially in Canada where everything is hard to find and also very expensive.

Partis Temporus: Allows someone to pass through a magical barrier.

Periculum: When you cast this spell, colored sparks will blast from your wand like a firecracker. (You can choose which color.)

Permanent Sticking Charm: Permanently glue something to a wall. Useful if you own a lot of paintings and live somewhere that has a lot of earthquakes.

Petrificus Totalus: When you cast this on someone they will stiffen straight and be unable to move and then usually fall over. This can cause a concussion so maybe don't cast it on people who are standing on a stone floor.

Piertotum Locomotor: Magically animate things like statues or suits of armor. Once they're "alive" the objects will follow your commands to their best of their abilities.

Point Me: Turn your wand into a compass that points north. This has limited applications and it's probably a better use of your time if you just summon a magical map since most maps have compass directions on them.

Prior Incantato: When you cast this spell on a wizard's wand, it will cause the wand to reveal the last spell that was cast with that wand. Like a very limited browsing history which can be wiped out by casting a simple spell like *Point Me*. So really only an inept wizard would ever get in trouble for casting something he wasn't supposed to.

Protean Charm: Basically a voodoo doll spell but for stuff instead of people. When you cast this on a group of similar objects, like chairs, and then break the leg off one chair, all the legs on all other chairs will be broken. Factory owners must live in constant fear of wizards sneaking into their assembly lines and casting this charm on their millions of identical widgets.

Protego: Cast this on yourself and if a villain tries to cast a curse, jinx, or hex on you, it will instead be cast on the villain. Basically the wizard version of: "I am rubber and you are glue, whatever you say bounces off of me and on to you." (There must be some sort of cool-down to prevent *Protego* abuse or everyone would be walking around protected all the time and curses, jinxes, and hexes would be useless.)

Protego Maxima: A protection spell that will block the negative effects of even the most powerful dark magic. This spell can be cast on a person, place, or thing, but only by a very powerful wizard or group of wizards.

Protego Totalum: Place a shield dome over a small area that will not allow anything to pass through. The only spell that can penetrate the shield is one of the unforgiveable curses: *Avada Kedavra, Crucio, or Imperio.* (Air can probably pass through the shield because of suffocation reasons. But that's it. Air and the unforgiveables. Nothing else.)

Quietus: If someone has magically enhanced their voice to be extremely loud and you're finding it super annoying, then cast this spell and their vocal chords will return to normal.

Reducio: Shrink something that has been magically enlarged. Probably a common spell cast in emergency rooms.

Reducto: Break an object in to smaller pieces, or even disintegrate it in to a millions of tiny pieces if you're feeling powerful.

Refilling Charm: Refills a glass/container with whatever liquid it originally contained. Economically speaking this is a dangerous spell since it can create a nearly unlimited supply of almost anything which would cause the price of that good to drastically fall destroying jobs and entire industries. Example: You could operate your restaurant with only a few bottles of expensive wine and just keep them refilling them over and over again. In the long run this would be beneficial for society since it frees the wine makers to do other things with their lives, but when introduced to an economy would create chaos overnight.

On the other side of the coin, some liquids like blood or medicine, are always in short supply, so it would be beneficial for wizards to flood the market. This spell creates an interesting ethical dilemma for wizards. If the blood bank runs out of a rare blood type, should the wizards magically refill the containers? Questions like this can be asked of most spells in the Harry Potter universe. If wizards have the power to intervene in Muggle affairs and save lives, do they have a moral obligation to do so? If wizards could have prevented World War 2 but chose not to, are they responsible, in part, for the millions of deaths? And even if they *had* intervened, are the wizards then responsible for all the technology that was never invented to win the war? Would Alan Turing ever have invented the early computer?

For the answer to these questions please consult an all-knowing entity. While you're talking to him/her/it, please ask them when the next *Game of Thrones* book is coming out. I can't even remember what happened in the last one. It's been like two thousand years.

Reparifors: A basic minor-healing spell that will cure most magical problems like paralysis, poison, itchy feet, or big runny booger nose.

Relashio: Causes your target to drop what they're holding. Can also be cast on objects to release a person from bindings. Don't cast this on a pregnant woman eating ice cream because when the dust settles you'll be in the hospital and she'll be in Azkaban.

Rennervate: This spell is used to wake people up who have been momentarily stunned. If your friend has been unconscious for more than a few minutes that's called a coma and is probably beyond the mending powers of *Rennervate*. Consult a doctor or make a new friend.

Reparifarge: Undo a magical transformation. Sometimes your chief tactical officer and your cook/space trader get merged in the transporter and become an annoying new entity called Tuvix. After a few plot points and commercial breaks you reach the conclusion that it's unethical to destroy two beings to create a third being and it has nothing to do with its aggravating superiority complex, so you use some transporter science to reverse the process. If you're a wizard though, instead of science you can use magic and cast *Reparifarge*, but since nobody understands how any of this crap works anyway what's the difference between science and magic? Nothing. That's partly why *Breaking Bad* was so good. Walter used actual science to solve his problems.

Reparo: Repair a simple object like a bowl or a cheap toaster your girlfriend knocked off the balcony because she'd smoked too much Longbottom Leaf and wanted to make toast while watching the sunset which was as she put it, "bluey purple and sorry about the toaster but it at least it didn't hit anybody."

Repello Inimicum: Protect your castle with this charm and disintegrate any villains trying to force themselves inside.

Revelio: This spell will reveal magically-concealed objects. It will also show you what someone's face looked like before their magic nose job.

Rictusempra: The tickle monster spell. Cast this one someone and watch as they collapse to the floor, overcome invisible hands tickling their entire body. Great spell for playing beer pong.

Rowboat Spell: Command a rowboat to magically row itself to a particular destination.

Sardine Hex: Causes sardines (tiny salted fish that taste great on pizza) to pour from your target's nose like Niagara Falls.

Scourgify: Use this on your dirty owl cage to magically clean it. Will also clean other things, like messy closets, antique stores, and that tuxedo you bought for weddings but only used once and now just hangs in your closet collecting dust and laughing at your inefficient spending habits.

Sectumsempra: Slash your target with magical energies as if you're swinging a sword into their flesh. This spell can cause serious and un-healable damage so don't go getting your ear chopped off or your brother will be making fun of you the rest of his life.

Self-Washing Dishes: Cast this spell on your plates and cutlery and you'll never have to leave them in the sink for a week while they "soak."

Shriveling Ears Curse: Cast this on a nice hat and then give the hat to someone and watch their ears shrivel up. Seems like a rotten thing to do but don't worry it's only temporary.

Silencio: Silence an animal or person so they can't speak or make any other type of noise. Probably a good spell to open with in a wizard duel.

Snow Blast: Command a pile of snow or snowballs to launch themselves at your target.

Sonorous Charm: Blast a giant sound wave from your wand. If cast strongly enough, will melt your opponent's face off.

Sonorus: If you cast this spell and point your wand at your neck, then your voice will be greatly magnified, like as though you were using a megaphone.

Specialis Revelio: When cast on a spell book, potion, or other magical devices, this spell will reveal any secret properties or hidden dangers. Probably a good spell to cast before you drink a potion you found on a skeleton's corpse in the ancient catacombs beneath a creepy medieval village.

Spongify: Make an object soft and sponge-like. Or, how to survive as a roadrunner if a coyote ties you to the train tracks and drops an anvil on your head.

Steleus: Cast this on someone and they will be overcome by sneezing as though it was allergy season and they were living in a house filled with long-haired cats, which most people agree are inferior to dogs.

Stinging Hex: Sting your target with an invisible stinger and cause them to break out in welts. Useful for distracting someone or making a scene on the subway between two strangers. "Did you just pinch my bum?" 'I certainly did not!' After they get thrown off the bus for fighting, use this opportunity to steal the better seat.

Stupefy: This spell will momentarily stun your target, and if cast powerfully enough can knock a person out.

Supersensory Charm: Temporarily enhances your basic senses so your Spider-Man costume appears more realistic.

Taboo: Curse a word or popular saying. Whenever someone utters the cursed words, you will be made aware of their location. Useful for tracking down runways, meddlesome kids, and bored 30-somethings on outdoor reality TV shows. (Mantracker cheats right? He has to be cheating.)

Tarantallegra: Aim this at someone and they will lose control of their legs and break out in a dance number.

Teleport Object: Use this spell to avoid paying ridiculous shipping fees on small objects like pencils, movies, and USB cables.

Tentaclifors: Sometimes I wonder what my girlfriend's head would look like if it were a giant purple tentacle. Now I know. It's not improvement.

Traitor Jinx: Cast this on someone after you make a deal or a pact with them. If they betray you then their skin will break out in boils and will spell SNEAK on their forehead.

Unbreakable Charm: Makes an object unbreakable. Cast this on your mother's expensive china and then drop it on the floor and watch her go from panic to relief to swatting you upside the head for being an idiot.

Unbreakable Vow: If you want to prove you're serious, then cast an unbreakable vow on the promise you just made. If you break your promise then you will die instantaneously. This spell makes shotgun weddings a lot more interesting.

Vanishing Fingers Jinx: Cast this spell on someone and giggle as you watch their fingers disappear.

Ventus: Blast your target with a strong gust of wind. Don't cast this spell too much or the effects could be environmentally disastrous due to the butterfly effect.

Vulnera Sanentur: Heal cuts, gashes, slashes, wounds, etc. Any lost blood will magically zoom back into the patient. A great spell to have on hand when you're doing that stupid knife trick where you stab between your fingers trying to impress a girl.

Wingardium Leviosa: Temporarily gain the powers of telekinesis, the ability to move objects with your mind.

Printed in Great Britain
by Amazon